FISH WISH

Bob Barner

Holiday House / New York

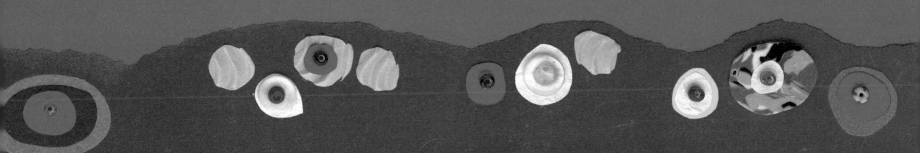

Library of Congress Cataloging-in-Publication Data
Barner, Bob.
    Fish Wish / Bob Barner.—1st ed.
    p.   cm.
    Summary: A young boy's dream sends him
on an underwater journey through a coral reef.
Includes factual information on coral reefs and
the animals that live in them.
    ISBN: 0-8234-1482-5 (hardcover)
[1. Coral reef animals Fiction. 2. Coral reefs
and islands.] I. Title.
PZ7.B2597Fi 2000
[E]—dc21 99-44491
CIP

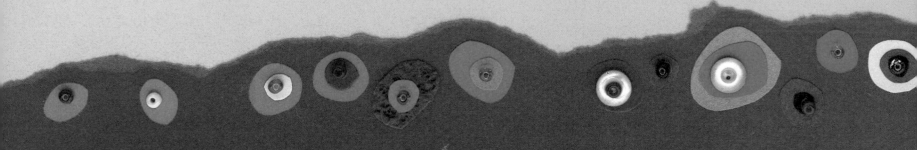

to Doug
and John

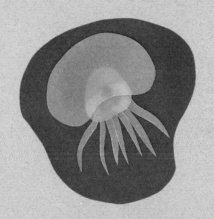

If I were a fish

I would wake up

on a coral reef.

Dolphins would pass above.

Sea turtles would glide by.

I would wind through octopus

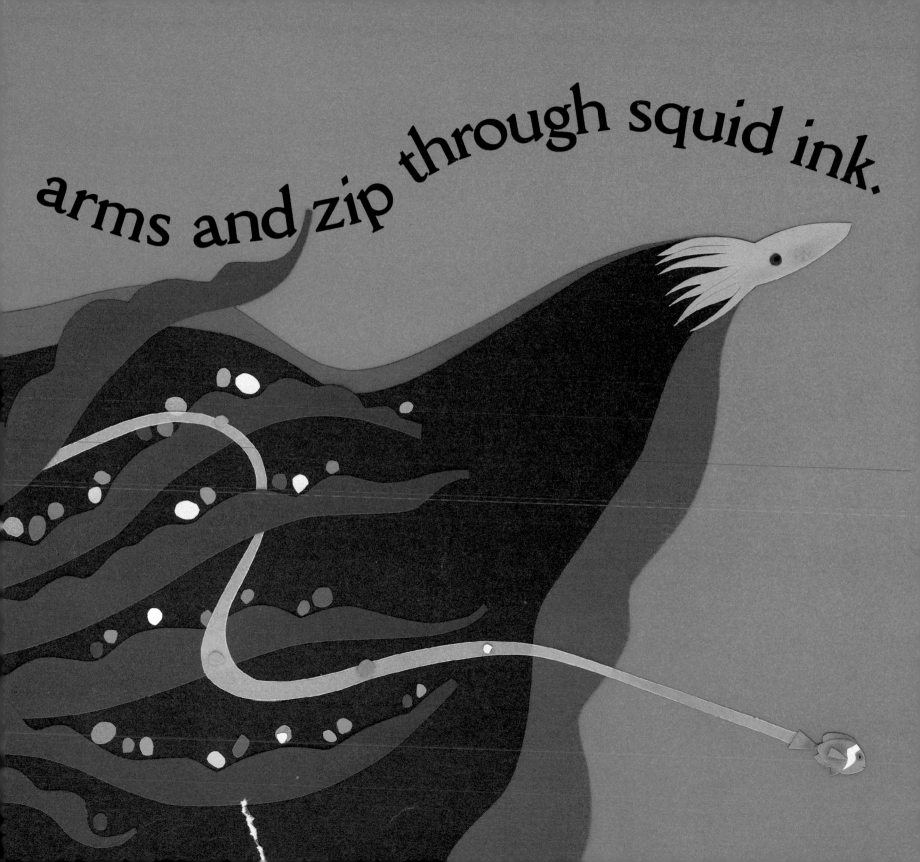

arms and zip through squid ink.

Sometimes I would dive

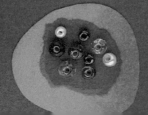

down deep

of jellyfish,

passing sea horses, shrimps,

and crabs.

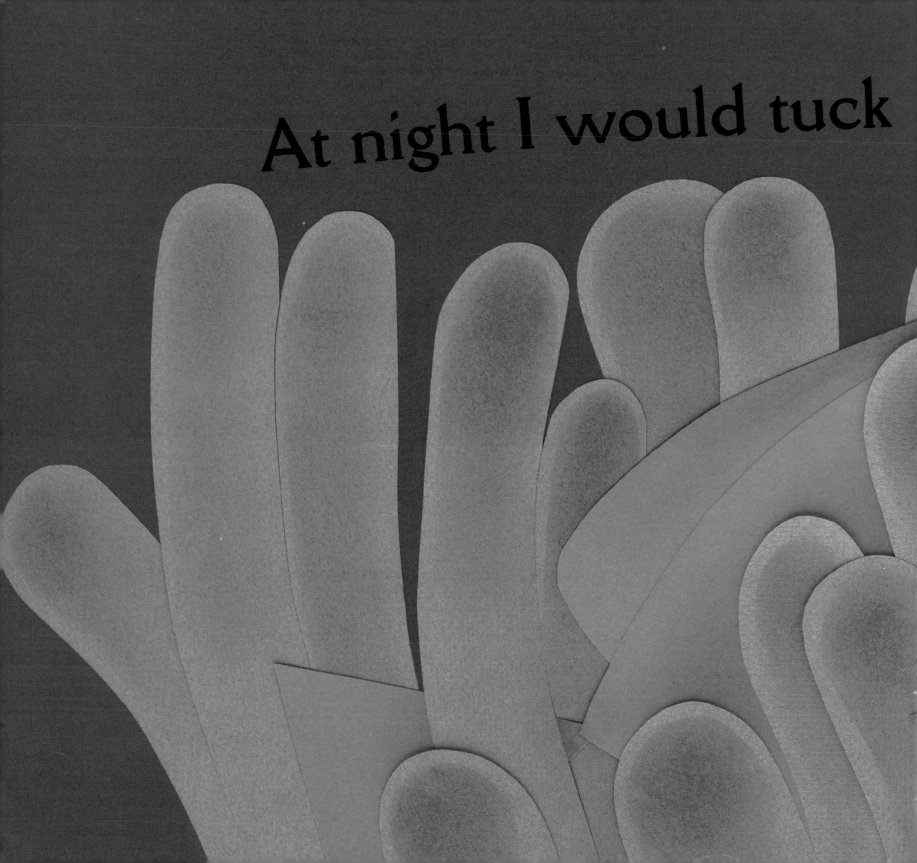

At night I would tuck

myself into a sea anemone,

and in a sea of stars

I would make a wish.

1. Sea Turtle
2. Squid
3. Dolphin
4. Trumpet Fish
5. Angelfish
6. Grouper
7. Moray Eel
8. Stingray
9. Shrimps
10. Barracuda
11. Clownfish
12. Sea Horse
13. Hermit Crab
14. Sea Cucumber
15. Giant Blue Clam
16. Octopus
17. Flounder
18. Sea Snake

Clownfish

Clownfish always live
near a sea anemone.
The anemone can sting
the clownfish's enemies with poison from its
tentacles that doesn't hurt the clownfish. The
clownfish scares away fish that would like to
take a bite out of the sea anemone.

Dolphin

Dolphins are mammals. They
breathe air through blowholes in the tops of
their heads. Dolphins can swim quickly through
the water by moving their powerful tails.

Squid

When squid are in danger, they
release a black ink-like fluid so they
can hide or escape. Giant squid
can be 50 feet long, but most are
much smaller. Some are only 2
inches long.

Octopus

The octopus has 8 arms.
When it is in danger, it
can change color to blend
in with the coral reef. The
smallest octopuses are
2 inches long;
the biggest are
30 feet wide.

Turtle

Sea turtles are reptiles and also
breathe air. Some kinds of sea
turtles grow up to 5 feet
in length. Some sea turtles
have lived 100 years
or more.

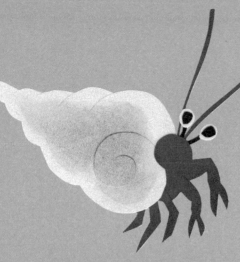

Hermit Crab

This little crab takes its house with it everywhere it goes! At the first sign of danger the crab pulls its body inside the shell. The largest hermit crabs are 1 foot long.

Shrimp

Some shrimps are as long as 9 inches, but most are much smaller. Shrimps live near the coral reefs in crevices or in burrows they dig in the sand.

Sea Horse

Sea horses are actually fish. They can be 2–8 inches in size. When sea horses are resting they can use their tiny tails to hold on to seaweed.

Jellyfish

Jellyfish are not fish. They float through the ocean, feeding on tiny plants and animals. Some are less than 1 inch wide; others are wider than 1 foot.

Starfish

Starfish are also called sea stars. They are not real fish. Starfish come in many shapes, sizes, and colors. Most starfish have 5 arms, but some have 10 or more.

Sea Anemone

Sea anemones look like flowers, but they are actually animals. They catch small creatures with their stinging tentacles, then stuff them in their mouths. Most sea anemones are 1–2 inches wide, but some are as wide as 3 feet.

THE CORAL REEF

A coral reef is built from the skeletons of tiny animals called corals. Corals live in clean, warm saltwater that allows sunlight to reach them. They look like plants, but they are actually animals that use their tentacles to catch and eat tiny sea creatures. Corals usually live together in large groups called colonies. Over thousands of years the skeletons of dead corals build up on top of one another to form a coral reef like the one in this book.

The beautiful colors we see in reefs are those of the living coral on top. All kinds of animals live in coral reefs, including the creatures in this book as well as sea slugs, giant blue clams, strawberry shrimp, lionfish, sea cucumbers, angelfish, lettuce slugs, brain coral, star coral, sea fans, and sand dollars. Coral reefs are home to thousands of species of marine plants and animals. New species are being discovered in coral reefs all the time.

These beautiful and fragile reefs of coral exist in the waters of 109 countries around the world. The Great Barrier Reef in Australia is 1,240 miles long, the largest in the world. Sixty percent of coral reefs are in the Indian Ocean and Red Sea, twenty-five percent are in the Pacific Ocean, and fifteen percent are in the Caribbean Sea. The Florida Keys in the United States have a long chain of reefs off the east coast of these islands.

Pollution, fishing, shell collecting, diving, and boating have damaged many reefs. We can all help protect the coral reefs by not polluting the water, by recycling, and by being careful to follow the rules if we have the chance to visit a beautiful, living coral reef.